TERROR IN PARADISE

V. J. Stovall

authorHOUSE®

AuthorHouse™
1663 Liberty Drive
Bloomington, IN 47403
www.authorhouse.com
Phone: 1-800-839-8640

First published by AuthorHouse 5/26/2010

ISBN: 978-1-4490-9829-2 (hc)
ISBN: 978-1-4490-9828-5 (sc)
ISBN: 978-1-4490-9830-8 (e)

Library of Congress Control Number: 2010907593

Printed in the United States of America
Bloomington, Indiana

This book is printed on acid-free paper.

**DEDICATED
TO THE MEMORY OF OUR
FALLEN SAILORS
WHO
DIED IN THE LINE OF DUTY
IN
SERVICE TO OUR COUNTRY**

PETTY OFFICER
FIRST CLASS
JOHN BALL

PETTY OFFICER
THIRD CLASS
EMIL WHITE

UNITED STATES
NAVY

UNITED STATES
NAVY

IN MEMORIAM - December 3, 1979

NSGA
Sabana
Seca

CTO1 John Ball

RM3 Emil White

TABLE OF CONTENTS

PREFACE

For many years, I have debated about publishing a memoir on the terrorist events of December 3, 1979. I kept the thoughts of this emotional event to myself and buried them in my soul for thirty years because I feared anger from my shipmates and repercussions from senior officers. I had made efforts to contact those parties involved in this event so they could present their own perspective, but I could not locate the individuals; those I was able to reach never returned responses most likely because they, too, buried the tragedy and moved on with their lives.

I addressed these concerns with my case manager and therapists at the Veteran's Clinic Mare Island, California. My therapist encouraged me to pursue this endeavor as a means of healing; bringing about closure to my pain; and reaching out to those shipmates effected by this incident.

The purpose of this memoir is to generate awareness to the American public that seventeen sailors, who were directly effected by the terrorist tragedy of December 3, 1979, will not be forgotten by their countrymen. Instead, they will be recognized for the sacrifices they made. Seventeen young people went through a horrific crisis that day and witnessed life and death in the flash of a second.

I pressed my therapist further about the emotional fall-out this memoir may have upon these sailors. She assured me that this publication would be a means to recognize and respect those sailors who had been forgotten over the years for their heroic efforts to protect and defend our country.

It is for this purpose that I put forth this publication to honor and recognize our countrymen for their sacrifice.

Lest we forget.

1 INTRODUCTION

Before I embark upon this memoir, let me introduce myself.

My name is Virginia Joy Stovall (nee: Thornton), but everyone in my life knows me by my middle name, Joy. I was born in Philadelphia, Pennsylvania, but I spent most of my youth in a strong Navy town, Pensacola, Florida.

I never had a strong desire to pursue a military career. I grew up in a Navy family and learned both the positive and the negative aspects of military life. My father, John William Thornton, was a retired Navy captain, who had a distinguished career as an officer. He was a man of great courage, honor and bravery and he received the second highest medal of our country, the Navy Cross. My father was a prisoner-of-war (POW) during the North Korean conflict from 1950-1953 and, later on in his career, he was instrumental in negotiations to win the release of many American POWs during the Vietnam years.

All of these attributes had a major impact on my decision as to whether I should (or should not) join the United States Navy. There were many downsides to a military career. There were many risks involved and, after my father endured the most brutal treatment by his captors in North Korea, I was concerned that such military risks and sacrifices, on a much different scale, would be too high a price for me to pay if I joined the military.

As a child, we moved frequently. It was difficult to transfer from one naval base to another every three to four years. I had developed friendships and relationships during those years just to have them severed upon our departure. My mother, Virginia Roberta Thornton, was the thread that held the tapestry of our family together. This was surely not an easy task for her; it was, perhaps, the greatest challenge she ever faced. She had endured three years of major worries about my father's disappearance and status in North Korea: was he MIA (missing in action); KIA (killed in action), or a Prisoner-of-War (POW)? This overwhelming feeling of limbo and anxiety during those three years never made her weak; instead, it made her strong. She was strong while raising a two-year-old son, my brother Jay, and reassuring him that Dad would come home soon. Jay would turn five once my father did come home.

Later on, in my youth, my mother would demonstrate that same strength. When I had those adolescent days and my emotions ran in every direction, I could always count on my mother's guidance. I felt secure knowing my mother was always accessible to me whenever I cried out for her.

Over the many years when my father served his country, I realized how truly strong he was. However, it was difficult for me to emotionally connect with him... He was always gone, sometimes, months at a time, and when he returned home, I felt I did not know this man who came into our home. There was an overwhelming feeling of detachment and, as a child, a void of emotion towards my father. This went on for many years and further drove a wedge in our father-daughter relationship.

All these aspects of military life spawned both fear and resentment in me and I was adamant with myself that I would never make the military service my career. I knew I wanted a family some day and I wanted my children to "know" me; I did not want to put my own children through separation anxiety that would result in their resentment and detachment from me. I did not wish to go through a second generation of these insecurities; I wanted my family to have roots, to have a foundation in one place we would call "home". I had decided once and for all that I would never, ever involve myself in the military....never say never, right??

When my father retired from the Navy in 1970, our family settled, once and for all, in Pensacola, Florida, where I remained until I......joined the United States Navy. Once my father was home for good, our relationship as a father and a daughter was established – it grew gradually. At the same time, I had matured and I began to appreciate why he served in the Navy and what he stood for and the many sacrifices he made to support his family and, on a broader scale, to serve his country.

When I entered my college years in Pensacola, Florida, I realized that soon I would be on my own and it was now my turn to establish a foundation for myself. Employment was not plentiful in Pensacola, Florida. When I realized that the only job opportunity for me to pursue was a military career, I enrolled in the Naval Reserve Officer Training

Corps (NROTC) at the University of West Florida in Pensacola, Florida. This program lasted for two years which consisted of orientation, physical training, navigation and engineering classes. The foundations of the NROTC program, coupled with my father's military experiences, prepared me for the challenges that lay ahead. After all, the Navy is not "just a job; it's an adventure!"

Upon my graduation from the University of West Florida in 1978, I was commissioned an officer in the United States Navy and sworn in by my father. This memorable event opened up new and exciting opportunities....and fears. I was a female in a male-dominated profession; I would receive orders which would send me to a naval base far away from friends and family. Then, the fear hit me head-on: "what are you thinking?"

My first duty station as a newly-commissioned ensign was the Naval Security Group Activity (NSGA) located at Sabana Seca, Puerto Rico. This was the start of an "adventure" I would never forget for the rest of my life.

(left)
Captain John William Thornton
United States Navy
Retired

(bottom)
Captain John Thornton
swearing me into the
United States Navy, June 1978

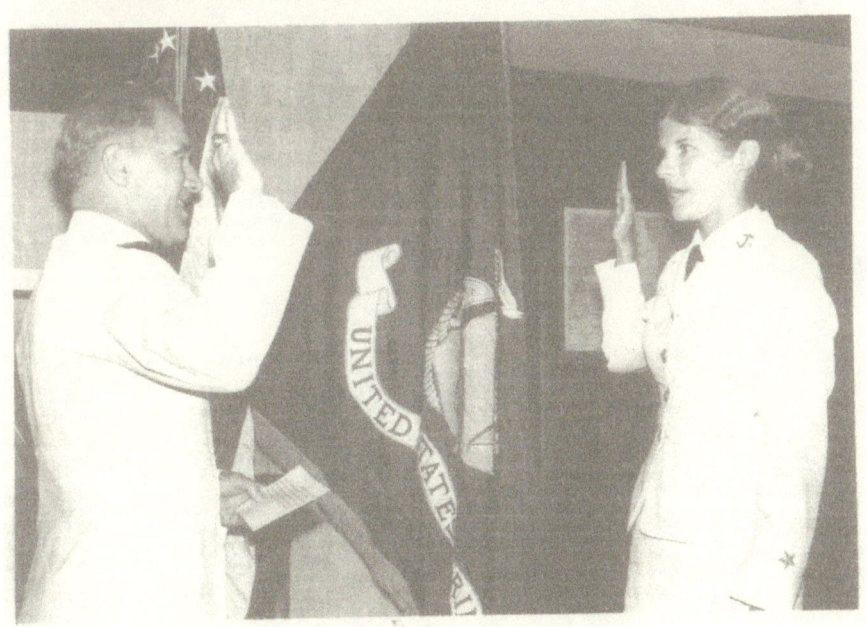

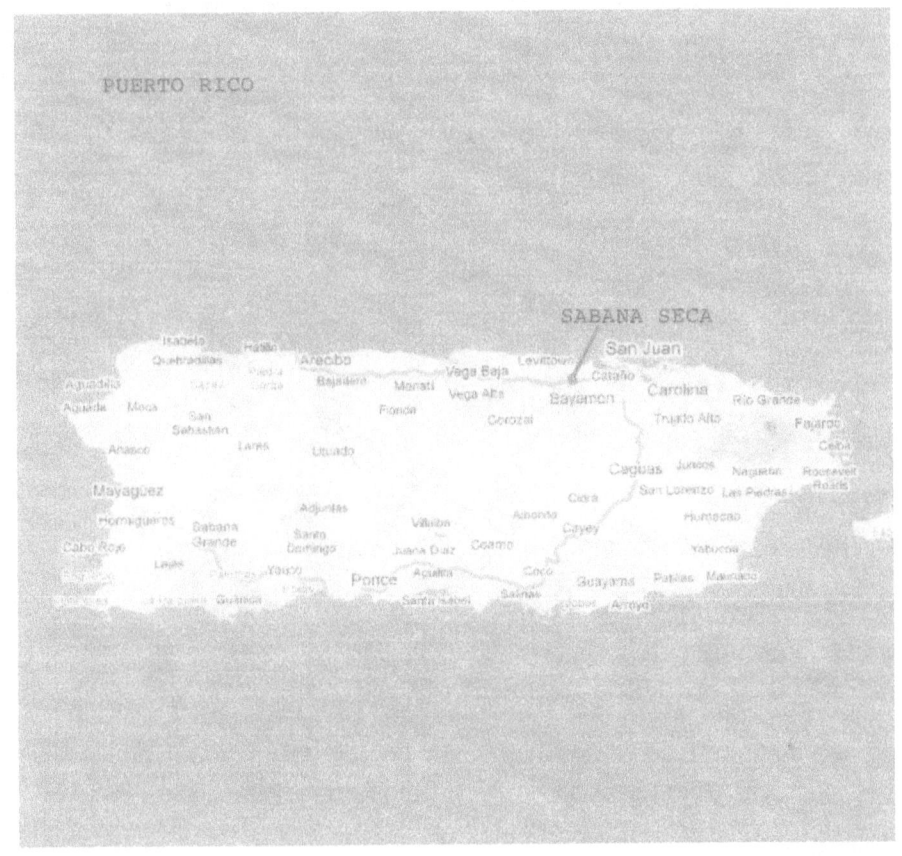

2 THE BUILD-UP

I reported to my first duty station in July 1978 not knowing what was in store for me. I knew my tour of duty would last two years and then I would be transferred to another naval base.

During my two-year tour, I was assigned numerous duties and collateral assignments ranging from Personnel Officer to Communications Officer; from Education Services Officer to Manager of the Officers' Mess to Community Relations Officer. The latter duty was, perhaps, my most rewarding of all as it allowed me to connect and interface with the Puerto Rican community. I already had a Bachelor of Arts degree (B.A.) in the Spanish languages and this enabled me to identify with the people right away knowing their language.

I encouraged our military personnel to step out of their comfort zone and start interfacing with the townspeople and enter their community. I had started up a "Basic Conversational Spanish" class onboard to help personnel "break the ice" with our civilian neighbors. Sadly, only a handful of "students" showed up for class. It would be a challenge to get both communities to come out of their shells and interface with one another.

Our community relations team did what we could to stimulate relations by hosting many social events both on and off our military installation. These events included barbecues, musical events, dances, sporting events and ceremonies to honor Puerto Rican veterans and civic leaders. As the weeks and months passed, relations between both communities grew closer.

All in all, the atmosphere was warm and positive and our actions of community outreach were further reciprocated as the small town of Sabana Seca made us feel welcome by hosting many events and inviting our participation in Christmas festivities and many more fun events. We truly grew together as one family, one community with no barriers to stop us from having fun; nothing at all.

One of many social events hosted   (third from left, front row)
by Mr. Martinez in Sabana Seca   Mr. Martinez
                                     (third from right, front row)
                                         Yours Truly

8

17

ARMED FORCES DAY
(l-r) Lucy Wrightson, YN1 Jaime Munoz; yours truly; CTI1
Ray Rodriguez

Commander Mike Werner, Commanding Officer, Mr. Ali Rivera,
director (musical group), Rondalla Cuerdas del Toa Baja and me

(top left) Lieutenant Bill Demente; (top right) yours truly, playing dominoes with members of the civilian community, Toa Baja (February 1980)

Memorial Day festivities honoring veterans, Catano, PR

Being an overly naïve and optimistic individual, I truly felt our communities had reached a pinnacle in our relationship with one another. All things were idyllic and all things were as tranquil and peaceful on this tropical island paradise. I never knew any dark side could exist on such a beautiful island filled with majestic beaches, warm surf and lush forests. How could this island ever have a dark side? To answer this question, one has to know a little about the history of Puerto Rico dating from 1898 to the present day.

Puerto Rico was originally named Boriquen or Borinquen, by the natives, and some townspeople will often go by the latter names. It was discovered by Christopher Columbus on November 19, 1493, and remained for the most part under Spanish rule until the end of the Spanish-American War. Puerto Rico was ceded to the United States under the terms of the Treaty of Paris, signed December 10, 1898.

The cause of Puerto Rican independence began not long after the United States took control of the island from Spain. It was not until World War 2 that Puerto Rican nationalists began a long string of terrorist attacks on both the island and the U. S. mainland.

Throughout the American years, politics focused largely on the question of "status". On one side, there had been a substantial group which desired statehood; on the other, was a far larger group which regarded statehood as impractical and impossible of attainment. In this group, there were those citizens who wanted outright independence, others who worked for independence with economic guarantees from the United States, and still others who settled for a form of autonomy or commonwealth as it exists today. In the 1998 vote, only about 2.5 percent of Puerto Ricans voted to become an independent country. Nevertheless, the Puerto Rican independence movement was the cause of some of the most dramatic terrorist acts in the United States in the second half of the twentieth century.

Militant Puerto Rican nationalism dates to the 1930s when Pedro Albizu Campos became president of the Puerto Rican Nationalist Party (NPPR), a political group advocating that Puerto Rico become a free and independent republic. The charismatic and Harvard-educated Campos injected the movement with a "radical nationalism", calling for "direct action" to achieve the goal of national sovereignty. He pledged that for every nationalist killed, a continental American would die—a promise he kept.

Independence movements remained non-violent for the most part, but this would change with the dawn of the Vietnam conflict and anti-imperialism sentiment that swept the world during the 1960s. This frenzy led to a revival of militant Puerto Rican nationalist groups such as the FALN (Fuerzas Armadas de Liberacion Nacional), the Macheteros (machete wielders); just to name a few. Radical groups joined forces during the late 1970s in solidarity for Puerto Rican independence by whatever means necessary.

3 THE AMBUSH

In order to fully understand how such a terrorist operation could be carried out, one needs to be familiar with the lay-out of our military installation.

Our base was located in two areas separated by approximately five miles of civilian residential housing and markets and a single-lane road (Route 867) connecting the two areas. Our operations site was, for the most part, located in a secluded, open field which housed our working men and women, who were known as "watchstanders". Our "watchstanders" consisted of three shifts (morning, noon and night) with a fifteen-minute overlap to

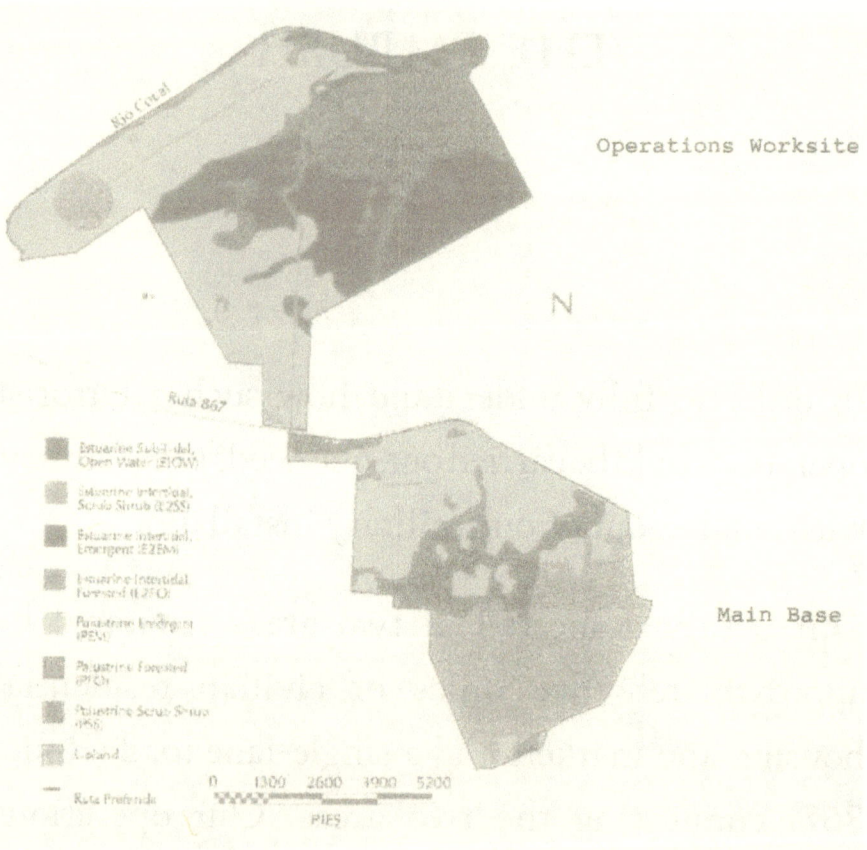

NAVAL SECURITY GROUP ACTIVITY SABANA SECA PUERTO RICO

effect a smooth transition. These fifteen minute periods allowed our watchsections time to receive operational debriefings, safety training and other events that were underway both on and off our base. These fifteen minutes were critical to many watchstanders who often felt isolated from the rest of the command and they, naturally, wanted to know what was going on and not be "left in the dark".

The single-lane road that connected both our Main Base to the Operations site was in poor condition and we were discouraged from using our own vehicles because of expensive damages we would incur. Instead, we made use of a school bus, one that would take both our watchstanders and our dayworkers to and from the operational site.

You will recall earlier on that I had mentioned that there was much political unrest, particularly when "statehood" was ever addressed. During local elections, "statehood" was often placed on the ballot and this caused an atmosphere of agitated excitement and anxiety amongst the townspeople.

Once again, there were open demonstrations from both sides in our neighboring communities; some were peaceful; some were not; one side in favor of making Puerto Rico our 51ˢᵗ state; the other side wanting independence. The majority of Puerto Rican voters overwhelmingly chose to remain a commonwealth.

There were those few citizens, however, who chose not to listen to the will of the people. Instead, these elements wanted to make their point known to their townspeople and to North American personnel, particularly those who wore "the uniform". Such groups, like the FALN, the Macheteros, and other radical groups decided to launch their own "campaign" to make their point known by whatever means necessary. These terrorist elements were determined to drive away the "military occupation" from "their country". They wanted to "rid their country" of those elements who "murdered" their comrades while they were "prisoners-of-war" in federal prisons. Retaliation was "their solution" to ridding their country of "Yankee imperialism" once and for all. The wheels were put into motion.

After carefully rehearsed planning and meticulous observations of our bus schedules; arrivals, departures and other movements, the terrorists were very familiar with our daily routine and used this knowledge to their advantage. They were now prepared to carry out their primary objective. The stage was set!

It was the morning of Monday, December 3, 1979. I woke up around 5:00 in the morning. I lived onboard the command in a residential unit at the Bachelor Officers' Quarters (BOQ). These quarters faced the baseball/football field which extended all the way out to the rickety road (Route 867) that our bus took each day/night to the Operations site. At approximately 6:30 in the morning, I was on the way downstairs from the BOQ heading over to the Administration building (called the Quarterdeck)

when I heard spontaneous popping sounds coming from the direction of the baseball field. At the time, I thought nothing about it as I thought it was simply fireworks being set off in celebration of the upcoming Holiday Season. This was not unusual as the local townspeople often would celebrate holidays, especially Christmas festivities, fireworks, barbecues etc. on a round-the-clock basis. I would discover later on that the "popping sounds" I heard were the actual gunfire from automatic weapons being fired into the bus, not the fireworks.

I proceeded to the Quarterdeck thinking it's just another Monday morning and that I would be facing another long week of assignments and tasks piling up in my in-basket.

Meanwhile, our bus had left the main base with its usual compliment of seventeen sailors on its way to the operational site to relieve the night-time watchstanders. There were altogether eleven males and six females onboard. One of the gentlemen, Petty Officer First Class (CTO1) John Ball, age

29, was the bus driver that morning. Originally from Madison, Wisconsin, Petty Officer Ball worked for me as supervisor of his watch section in the Communications Department. He was a very conscientious sailor and he placed as much dedication into his work as he did into his family. What I particularly recall of Petty Officer Ball, outside his strong commitment to his command, was his involvement in church activities and his marriage encounter groups. He was an amazing athlete who ran in many marathons and in other community-sponsored sporting events. The other gentleman, Petty Officer Third Class (RM3) Emil White, age 20, was from Charlotte Amalie, Virgin Islands. He was another sailor who was dedicated to his job. He was a lively, outgoing young man who brought a smile to every face with his witty sense of humor. His shining personality brought enlightenment to our command. He had an incredible talent for building radios and broadcasting. Petty Officer White would often host disco shows onboard our little base which brought many of our military "family" of approximately 250 people together. Petty Officer

White had great aspirations of establishing his own radio broadcasting station back home in his native Virgin Islands. He had even shown me the intricate details, designs and blueprints of his radio station----his dream that he had hoped would become a reality after he left the service. Petty Officer White was now riding that fateful bus seated directly behind the driver, Petty Officer Ball.

…..yes, it was a typical Monday morning. The bus with its unarmed personnel was on its way to the Operations site. Riding the bus for our sailors was a time for bonding over family outings and discussions about their career goals. In many ways, it gave the sailors the opportunity to ride together as a group, as a team, and more importantly, as a "family" like I addressed earlier. Here are our sailors embarking on their jobs to serve their country. Here are our sailors laughing and exchanging their thoughts about the activities they did over their break….just another day…..just another watch…..just the usual.

As the bus traveled along Route 867 to the operational site, an olive-green pick-up truck suddenly pulled out from the right side of the road and blocked the bus' path. This was followed by the sudden appearance of a white van coming from the opposite direction stopping parallel to the bus. A bus with no versatile mobility to maneuver safely on such a narrow, shaky road was now stopped in its tracks. As quick as a flash, yet well-rehearsed, unidentified gunmen from the surrounding vehicles commenced firing indiscriminately into the bus with automatic/semi-automatic weapons. Glass shattered everywhere with richoche-ing gunfire in all directions. Petty Officers Ball and White were hit instantaneously and killed; ten other sailors suffered multiple injuries – some critical! At no time did any of the unidentified gunmen ever enter the bus which would have surely resulted in more lives lost. Confident that the unidentified gunmen had achieved their primary objective, they took off as quickly as they had arrived.

In the midst of this chaos, a courageous chief petty officer, CTRC Warren Smith, used quick thinking to get his troops to remain silent for fear that the gunmen may come onboard to finish what they started. In spite of his serious wounds, Chief Petty Officer Smith took control of this spontaneous crisis by getting behind the driver seat, where Petty Officer Ball had sat just seconds before, and somehow was able to miraculously maneuver the bullet-ridden bus over the narrow road, u-turned, and quickly returned to base. His quick actions allowed the injured to receive immediate medical attention and he was, thus, instrumental in saving lives.

Upon arrival at the Quarterdeck, I observed confusion coming from all directions. Helicopters arrived landing in our open field—sirens everywhere. I walked in the Quarterdeck and observed our newly-arrived officer, an ensign, who had just inherited her first watch as Command Duty Officer (CDO). (All officers onboard our command had primary assignments and collateral duties, but at the same time, we were assigned watch duties as CDOs. These positions were assigned to each of us on a rotational basis to act on behalf of our Commanding Officer when he was not on duty). This young ensign was overwhelmed, frantically making entries into the logbook as events spontaneously unfolded around her. The Commanding Officer, now arriving, observed the young officer in action, then looked at me and said, "You're in charge!" Needless to say, I was caught off-guard and was, myself, overwhelmed by the magnitude of this tragedy and the responsibility of operations now placed upon me. I had been onboard the Sabana Seca base for eighteen months, an ensign myself, twenty-three years old, and now here I was in a state of shock. There was no time for emotion; no time to question. My primary responsibility was to do damage control and attempt to restore our command to normal as quickly as possible:

As Communications Officer, I was responsible for preparing the required flash message and OPREP BLUE reports (similar to "breaking news" bulletins) that required immediate dispatch reaching the highest levels in our government.

Our original three watchsection teams had to be immediately reconfigured into port/starboard, two watchsection teams since our third watchsection had now been immobilized.

I had to piece together all events leading up to the attack and investigate the aftermath of this tragedy. The damaged bus, now setting by our Quarterdeck, needed to be examined for our logbooks. Being careful not to touch anything that would compromise criminal evidence, I was able to make out fragments of bullets, shells and casings and multiple bullet holes particularly on the left side/driver side of the bus. There was much blood in the area where both the driver and his passenger behind him had sat. The smell of death was surrounding me and I felt completely motionless. The smell remains vivid to this day in my mind, heart and soul.

Medical staff reported the status of our personnel identifying the deceased and injured, as follows:

CTO1 John R. Ball (deceased)
RM3 Emil E. White (deceased)

CTRC Warren Smith (wounded)

CTT2 Cynthia C Edwards (wounded)

CTO3 Sandra L. Seaton (wounded)

CTM3 Joseph R. Key (wounded)

CTRSA Monique A. Ritter (wounded)

CTRSN Bradley D. Clark (wounded)

RM3 Dottie A. Allen (wounded)

CTRSN Allen Bush (wounded)

CTOSN Richard D. Sauter (wounded)

CTM2 Debra J. Whitehurst (wounded)

CTRSN Clifton Looney

RM3 Drusilla Penderghest

CTM2 Robert Minnick

CTM3 Gilbert Zuback II

CTTSN Kenneth Toman

The medical staff reported that there was only one body bag in our small clinic on base. We were relieved to observe the immediate arrival of the MEDIVAC choppers who had the necessary equipment to airlift our comrades. It was over-whelming to realize that two conscientious, active men I had just seen the day before, were now gone. I had to squelch my emotions and feelings because I was "in charge".

The Marine Detachment onboard our command launched reactionary patrols to keep our personnel safe and secure while, at the same time, seeking out and locating those responsible for this atrocity and bringing them back to face justice.

Perhaps, most overwhelming of all were the news personnel and news agencies from around the world that descended upon us. They gathered outside the gates and appeared to be in a "feeding frenzy" demanding to know what had happened because it was "their right" to report to the public what had happened. Our Public Relations Officer (PAO) was called upon to handle this crowd and inform them that no names or circumstances would be released until the next of kin would be properly notified. Due to a poor, out-dated phone network in Puerto Rico, frantic calls to loved ones were not getting through and when the phone lines were overloaded, the lines would subsequently crash. It took about six to eight hours to finally reach RM3 White's family who resided in the Virgin Islands.

Status reports on our personnel were coming in on the seriously wounded personnel. One young lady, who had been declared deceased upon arrival at the hospital was revitalized by medical personnel. This was the only bright light I experienced on this awful day. Regrettably, her unborn baby was lost and now, a third person, became the latest victim of this atrocity.

There was multiple confusion upon arrival of various law enforcement agencies: FBI, NIS, ATF, local police, just to name a few. All of these agencies, however conscientious they may have been, had their own agenda as to how to approach this investigation. Critical information was not exchanged; no networking of any kind. There was no real cohesion; just confusion and frustration. As a result, it gave the terrorists the opportunity to go back underground. Whatever cases investigators may have "resolved" pertaining to this incident did not hold up in court. Consequently, suspects were released. I personally spoke to the Puerto Rican police from the neighboring town of Toa Baja and

I found that they were more knowledgeable because they knew the territory, the people and were the best resource we so critically needed. However, the powers-that-be were critical that we were not more receptive to our government law enforcement agencies who were advanced in their techniques of investigations as opposed to the locals.

So, who was responsible for this atrocity? We were always wary of local elections whenever statehood was placed on the ballot. There was much dissent in some Puerto Rican communities who wanted the American military presence off the main island and, more specifically, the neighboring island of Viequez. The people of Viequez were understandably agitated because their island was frequently used by both Navy and Marine Corps forces as a bombing range in addition to amphibious training and military exercises.

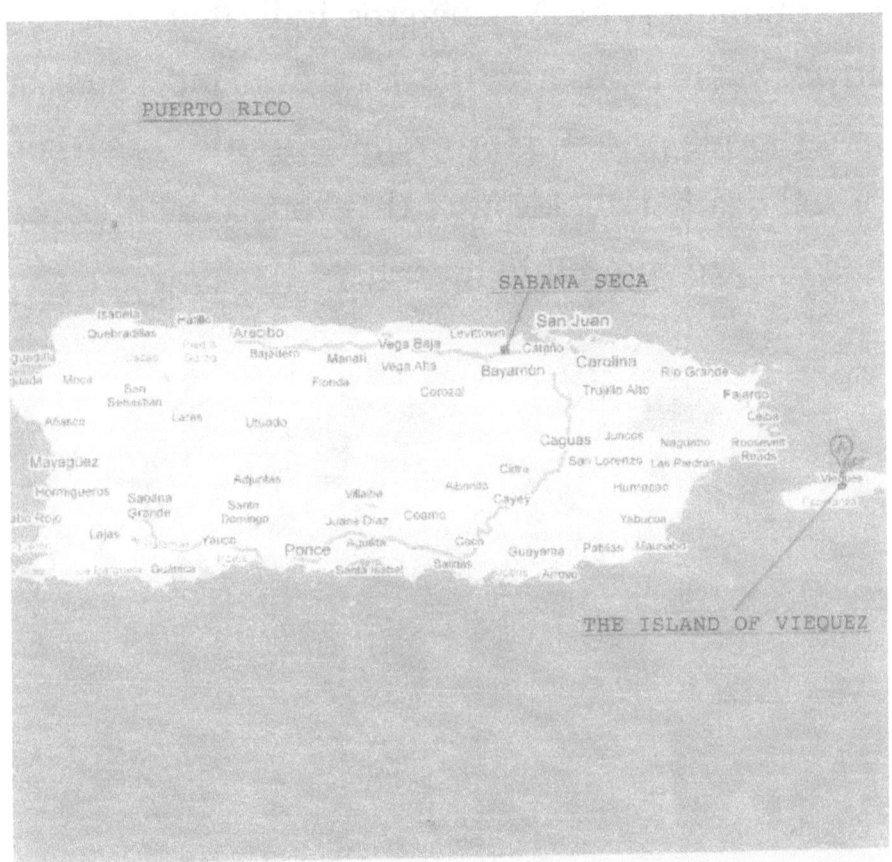

The Island of Viequez was used by naval forces as a bombing range and was the cause of much unrest among the civilian population...and was the fuel to ignite the passion of the independista movement

Naval presence on Viequez ended in May 2003

These factors, among others, became the fuel of independista terrorist groups, like the Macheteros, who claimed responsibility for our tragedy. In the communiqué, the Macheteros indicated that the attack was in reprisal for the death of an independista in a Florida prison. However, authorities ruled the prison death a suicide after they found the prisoner had hanged himself in his cell.

The actual written communique addressing responsibility for
the attack on December 3, 1979. English translation follows

3 de diciembre de 1979.
San Juan, Puerto Rico.

En la mañana de hoy 3 de diciembre fuerzas conjuntas de la
Organización de Voluntarios para la Revolución Puertorriqueña (OVRP),
el Ejército Popular Boricua (EPB-MACHETEROS) y las Fuerzas Armadas
de Resistencia Popular (FARP) llevaron a cabo una acción militar
contra las fuerzas militares yankis de ocupación que operan en la
Base Naval de Inteligencia (U.S. NAVAL SECURITY GROUP ACTIVITY) en
el barrio Sabana Seca del pueblo de Toa Baja.

Las agresiones imperialistas contra nuestro pueblo han sido una
constante que en los últimos años han culminado con la masacre de
dos jóvenes patriotas en el Cerro Maravilla y más recientemente con
el asesinato de un joven agricultor y patriota, Angel Rodríguez
Cristóbal, en las masmorras federales de Talahasee, Florida.

El asesinato de Angel Rodríguez Cristóbal fue perpetrado por la
inteligencia yanki para intimidar a nuestro pueblo y a sus dirigentes,
en un vano intento para que cesemos en nuestra lucha. En vez de
sentirse intimidado, nuestro pueblo responde con verguenza e indignación.

La confabulación entre el gobierno colonial, principal verdugo
en el asesinato del Cerro Maravilla, y el gobierno norteamericano,
ejecutor de Rodríguez Cristóbal, es evidente. Persistiendo en su
afán imperialista de perpetuar el control y explotación de nuestro
pueblo pretenden paralizar las fuerzas patrióticas en su avance liber-
tario y revolucionario mediante una política de terror y represión.

No se llamen a engaño los estrategas militares yanquis. La
sangre de los mártires y patriotas boricuas será cobrada con la sangre de los imperialistas. Las fuerzas armadas de ocupación yanqui
serán blanco del fuego patriota, en grado superlativo, cada vez que
la mano asesina del imperialismo ciegue la vida de un patriota puerto-
rriqueño.

Le advertimos a los imperialistas yanquis que deben respetar la
vida y la seguridad de nuestros prisioneros de acuerdo a la Conven-
ción de Ginebra sobre la guerra. De lo contrario, serán responsables
de las consecuencias irreversibles del accionar que se produzca como
resultado de la indignación popular.

Las organizaciones clandestinas que suscribimos este comunicado
no estamos jugando a la guerra. Estamos dispuestos a llevar esta
lucha hasta sus últimas consecuencias.

¡POR LA INDEPENDENCIA Y EL SOCIALISMO, VIVA PUERTO RICO LIBRE!

December 3, 1979
San Juan, Puerto Rico

On the morning of December 3, forces from the Volunteer
Organization for the Puerto Rican Revolution (OVRP), the People's
Boriquen Army (Macheteros) and the Armed Forces of Popular
Resistance (FARP) jointly carried out military action against
the occupation of Yankee military forces which operate in
the Naval Intelligent Base (U S Naval Security Group Activity)
in Sabana Seca, suburb of Toa Baja.

The imperialist aggressions against our people have been con-
tinuous and constant for the last several years and have
culminated with the masacre of two patriotic youths in Cerro
Maravilla and, more recently, the murder of a young fieldworker
and patriot, Angel Rodriguez Cristobal, in the federal prison
of Tallahassee, Florida.

The murder of Angel Rodriguez was perpetrated by Yankee intelligence as a means to intimidate our people and our leaders and
in a vane attempt to stop us from our struggle.Instead of feeling
intimidated, our people responded with shame and indignation.

The corroboration between the colonialist government, the main
executioner in the Cerro Maravilla murder; and the NorthAmerican
government, who murdered Rodriguez Cristobal is evident in their
persistent imperialistic goal of perpetuating the control and
exploitation of our people. They pretend to paralyze the patriotic forces in their libertarian and revolutionary advancement
through political terror and repression.

Do not allow yourselves to be deceived by the Yankee military
strategists. The blood of our martyrs and boriquen patriots
will have to be paid with the blood of the imperialists. The
Yankee-occupying military forces will be the target of an em-
passioned patriot, who willingly, will assasinate the hand of
imperialism who ends the life of a Puerto Rican patriot.

We are warning Yankee imperialists that they must respect the
life and security of our prisoners in accordance with the
Geneva Convention. Otherwise, they will be responsible for the
irreversible consequences and actions that might come out as a
result of the popular indignation.

The clandestine organizations offer this communique to state
we are not playing in this war. We are committed to take this
struggle to its ultimate consequences.

FOR INDEPENDENCE AND SOCIALISM, LONG LIVE A FREE PUERTO RICO!

THE ACTUAL CRIME SCENE AS PROVIDED TO INVESTIGATORS

December 3, 1979

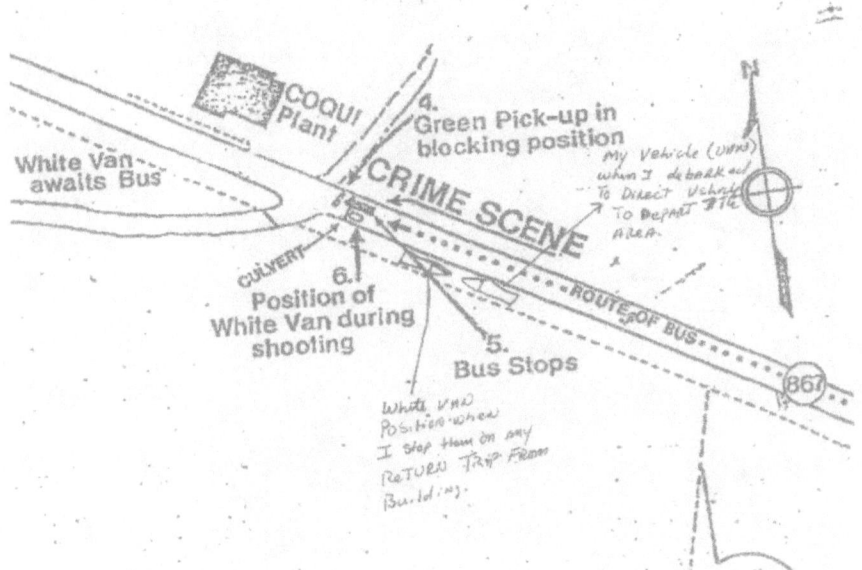

The actual vehicles used by the terrorists in the attack on our unarmed bus (December 3, 1979)

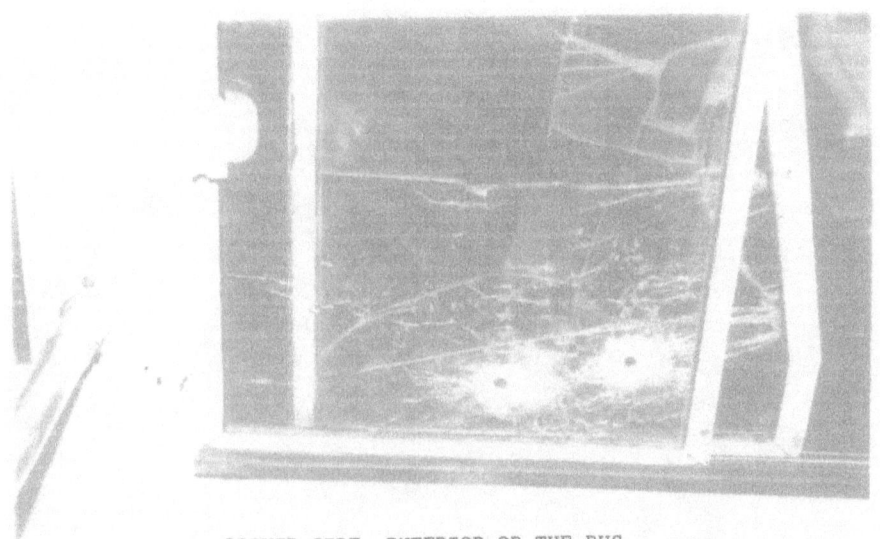

DRIVER SIDE, INTERIOR OR THE BUS

RIGHT SIDE OF BUS IMMEDIATELY AFTER THE SHOOTING

BULLET ENTRY TAGS, TAPED TO THE BUS

CLOSE-UP OF TAPED BULLET ENTRY TAGS, NUMBERED

Based on a congressional report on terrorism by Representative Dan Burton (cerca 1999), the following information was gathered on the motives of the Macheteros:

Former Macheteros member Carlos Rodriguez implicated Juan Segarra Palmer, who was granted clemency by President Bill Clinton, in the attack on the Navy bus. Rodriguez told authorities that he attended a Macheteros meeting in mid-November 1979 at which time Segarra made an announcement that the Macheteros would attack a Navy bus. The group had discussed attacking other military installations; however, it dismissed those plans in favor of the Navy bus. Segarra planned and instructed others on the operation, including the orders to shoot at the bus from a moving vehicle, while blocking the bus with another vehicle. The Macheteros met three weeks after the attack to discuss the operation. During the meeting, Segarra evaluated the attack and commented that "while the operation had resulted in two dead, he felt the results should have been more severe".

There were no resolutions in place to put this tragedy behind us. Our command was at the point where we needed to move forward.

In response to the ambush, our Commanding Officer, Commander Mike Werner, ordered our Marine Corps detachment to escort our sailors to and from the worksite to relieve our watchstanders, daily and nightly. Additionally, police officials from our neighboring communities also provided escort protection. Those who chose to drive their own vehicles did so at their own risk. We were strongly advised to wear civilian clothes to and from the worksite to detract attention. Upon arrival at our worksite, we changed into our uniforms. This process went on for several weeks.

The challenges I faced as the Community Relations Officer for our command was trying to re-boot our relationship with our Puerto Rican neighbors before prejudicial racial-profiling, anger and scapegoating would set into our minds and consume our souls. I had very close ties to the Puerto Rican community, but they were now uneasy and uncertain following the aftermath of this tragedy. The local townspeople were worried about retaliation and chastisement from our military personnel.

Our Puerto Rican "family" was just as offended and appalled by the actions of the terrorists responsible for this atrocity. The community went so far in erecting a sign at the shooting site that stated, "The people of Puerto Rico apologize to the U. S. Navy personnel in the bus on 3rd December 1979", followed by the listing of our deceased and injured sailors. I assured our townspeople that the perpetrators, the Macheteros and other radical groups, were not representative of the Puerto Rican people; they were terrorists who had their own agenda to undermine the will of the Puerto Rican people.

As the healing process was put into action, we sponsored many social events as did our local townspeople in efforts to bring our communities together. We got back to "normal" as quickly as we could: we continued with our mission, we cared for our families and cared for one another. We still went on with our Christmas holiday festivities; our theatre and rock band continued to perform on stage; our children went to school and we still went out into a welcoming community. John Ball and Emil White, our fallen sailors, would have wanted us to move forward.....and so we did!

Most significantly, our command hosted a tribute to celebrate the lives of our two fallen shipmates. This event was a dedication ceremony in which two of the buildings on the base were named in their honor:

The Command's Enlisted Club after Emil White

The Command's Gym Complex after John Ball

THE COMMAND''S GYM COMPLEX NAMED FOR JOHN BALL

THE COMMAND'S ENLISTED CLUB NAMED FOR EMIL WHITE

SIGN OF APOLOGY ERECTED BY THE SHOOTING SITE

WHITE CROSS ERECTED BY SHOOTING SITE

The future and mission of Naval Security Group Activity Sabana Seca diminished greatly as the years passed. The United States Navy found itself in a position to begin downsizing its forces and streamlining operations throughout our country and the world. The decision to close NSGA Sabana Seca was hastened by the arrival of Hurricane Georges. This storm slammed into Puerto Rico severely damaging the operational site with high winds and heavy floods in 1999. The damages to the operational site were extensive and the costs to repair the facility far exceeded the costs the Navy would pay so it was later determined that there was no longer any justification to keep the base open. When our operational mission was phased out, Naval Security Group Activity Sabana Seca closed its doors in January 2003. The remaining commands on the island were decommissioned and naval presence in Puerto Rico ended in 2004.

4 LESSONS LEARNED

I mentioned earlier that there was much confusion when various law enforcement agencies arrived at the scene. Many of these agencies gathered much information and evidence, but there was a lack of networking between these organizations. Every one of these elements had their own agenda and their own modus operandi to pursue our case, but there was little cooperation to UNIFY all critical information quick enough to bring the terrorists to justice. As a result, the perpetrators had the opportunity to go underground and any information that was successfully gathered by law enforcement was either inadmissible in court or insufficient to bring forth a conviction beyond a reasonable doubt. In the end, the Federal Bureau of Investigation (FBI) closed the books on this case in 1993.

Over the next several years, the Macheteros took credit for many attacks on policemen and military posts, including the destruction of eleven Puerto Rican Air National Guard planes in January 1981, at a cost of $45 million. Eventually, most of the members of both organizations were arrested and jailed, and the wave of Puerto Rican nationalist terrorism ended....for now. In September 1999, President Bill Clinton released sixteen terrorists by granting them clemency in exchange for their rejection of violence.

Once again, the lack of coordination and cooperation among law enforcement organizations would recur in the aftermath of September 11, 2001, but on a much larger scale. The citizens and their families of those who suffered in 9/11 demanded an answer and requested a special congressional commission to investigate and evaluate the failures. This commission identified specific areas and offered recommendations. There was surely the need to have agencies share their critical intelligence-gathering with other agencies in an expedient manner to decrease the chances of terrorist attacks.

After much discussion on this matter, legislation was underway to recommend establishment of one law enforcement agency to oversee the threat of terrorism. This agency would encompass and streamline the missions of all law enforcement agencies whose sole objective would be to secure the United States from terrorist threats or attacks. On October 8, 2001, President George W. Bush issued an executive order creating the Office of Homeland Security (OHS). The mission of the office was to develop and coordinate the implementation of a comprehensive national strategy to secure the United States from terrorist threats or attacks. The office was charged with coordinating the executive branch's efforts to detect, prepare for, prevent, protect against, respond to, and recover from terrorist attacks within the United States and its territories. Members in this Office include the Directors of the FBI, CIA and Federal Emergency Management Agency (FEMA); the Attorney General; the Secretaries of Defense, Health and Human Services, Transportation and Treasury; and any other officers of the executive branch designated by the president. The OHS was to ensure coordination of homeland security-related activities of executive departments and agencies, and the development and implementation of homeland security policies.

More than forty agencies and offices are responsible for domestic security. The challenge before the OHS was to coordinate and organize these disparate entities, which may have different mandates and goals, are geographically widespread, and may see themselves in competition with each other, into an efficient organization capable of devising successful anti-terrorist strategies. Communication is the greatest hurdle: information collected by one agency may not be routinely shared with others, computer systems can be incompatible, and public announcements can contradict one another.

The OHS established a national coordination center a few miles from the White House. The center's goal is to improve information sharing and coordination among federal agencies, and would include state and local agencies. The OHS agenda includes plans to further develop the border security agency; revamping collection and distribution of intelligence; creating national homeland security performance standards for federal, state and local agencies, particularly first responders including police and firefighters; creating a national alert system; and encouraging private industry to improve security.

The establishment of this consolidated law enforcement agency is a major step in the right direction to help us combat terrorism. It remains to be seen, however, if this agency will be successful in assuring all Americans that we are truly safe from terrorism once and for all….only time will tell.

5 REFLECTIONS

After all these events, trials and tribulations, how does one begin to understand and process a tragic event that occurred thirty years ago? What is this overwhelming emotion that suddenly, after many years of passage, hits one so hard, you feel as if you are going to faint and wake up hoping the event was simply a nightmare?

These questions are hard to process rationally and the need for counseling and therapy are paramount to "walk one through" this dark tunnel to hopefully see that bright light ahead. There are no clear answers to grapple with this tragedy of December 3, 1979, at NSGA Sabana Seca, Puerto Rico.

My own memories of this tragedy are just the tip of the iceberg compared to the memories of those sailors who suffered far worse than I did on the bus that fateful morning. By far, their memories go beyond the scope of my own. I would not even begin to address their thoughts, pains or emotions on the subject. I would say clearly that their resilience to this unfortunate event was amazing. Many of the sailors from the bus returned to work with the same drive, dedication and commitment they always had. They had proven to many of us that moving forward, not looking back, is a healthier approach to daily living.

Nevertheless, the aftermath of this tragedy has haunted me for a long time, but I was forced to bury this pain and move on; to not look back—ever! After all, I was a Naval Officer, a cryptologic officer with multiple security clearances; a command duty officer (CDO). I was in the "official" capacity where critical decisions had to be spontaneously made without emotional inhibitors to cloud my judgment. Feelings and emotions about events as they unfolded before me were not permissible as they would interfere with decision-making and render me incompetent to perform my duties.

As a Naval Officer and being only one of two female officers attached to the navy base during this tragedy, the stress and pressure placed upon me was overwhelming to say the least. Our Commanding Officer made it very clear to his personnel that noone was to speak of this event, particularly while it was under investigation and given the fact that our command operated somewhat incognito due to the highly-classified mission we carried out. Maintaining a low profile limited our visibility and exposure to the outside world and, thus, we could continue our mission without distraction from the public.

……but the "distraction" within me kept building up. We were discouraged by superiors to seek out any kind of medical/psychiatric help because such treatment would "expose" us to the outside world which would seriously compromise our mission. Officers, like me, feared we would be labeled as "psychologically unfit/incompetent to fulfill our duties as commissioned officers". Such a diagnosis would have resulted in loss of security clearances, which in effect, would have cost me my promotions and my career as a cryptologic officer.

So, I never said a word and went on (or TRIED to go on) as if nothing had ever happened.....

.....as the years passed, it seemed like those memories were dust in the wind, but then about twenty years after the incident, I was channel-surfing on the television and stumbled across a film that contained a scene that brought the pain back. This particular scene was from the movie, "Battle for the Planet of the Apes". The scene consisted of human mutants riding a school bus to a particular destination when, suddenly, an armed group of weapon-carrying gorillas encircled the bus and opened fire on the passengers killing everyone onboard. This particular movie scene would, under normal circumstances, not have any effect on anyone, but when I saw this scene, I found myself hyperventilating, sweating and crying hysterically. The memories had completely engulfed me.

From that point on, I could never board a school bus for fear of seeing the blood of my comrades, my friends, on the bus. I see my son joyfully riding a school bus, but when I approach a school bus to retrieve my son, I must "cover" and conceal my fears as I do not want my son to see his mother unravel before his eyes. Additionally, when I hear fireworks (or any kind of popping noise), without question, I hit the ground fearing I may be the next one shot.

I did not know how to handle any of this because it had been reinforced and "grounded" into me that going to a doctor would result in my being labeled a "nut", "misfit", "unstable" or worse, a "psychopath". I found myself blaming myself...ashamed of myself to feel the way I felt...to feel WEAK because I was indeed a Naval Officer, a leader in charge and strong in what I was tasked to do. After all, what would MY FATHER say about such weakness? What would he think of me?? My father would think of me as weak and with no backbone and a total disgrace to the uniform of a naval officer.

Then, another national tragedy hit, which further opened up my emotional wounds: September 11, 2001. The monolithic fall-out from this event triggered the events of December 3, 1979, and once again, I found myself in despair and reliving the nightmare all over again. From that day on, I was deeply effected by the magnitude of this horrific attack on our American soil and all its elements that went along with this: the terrorists; the communiqués; no regard for human life; airplanes as weapons; and finally, the shock that 9/11 had on all of us and how it changed our country forever.

From that day on, I could no longer "bury" the pain of both terrorist tragedies. What's a veteran to do??

I picked myself up and went to the Veterans' Administration Outpatient Clinic at Mare Island, California, to seek out psychiatric help because I could not comprehend that after all the success I had in burying these events, suddenly I could no longer do so. Both my therapist and psychiatrist agreed that what I was suffering from was a condition called post-traumatic stress disorder (PTSD). So, what is PTSD?

As defined by Dr. Mark Goulston, MD, and former assistant clinical professor of psychiatry, UCLA, PTSD is a major, life-altering disorder that strikes many people who survive traumatic experiences. Millions of people of every age and in every walk of life are affected and many of them suffer alone and in silence. They feel scared, anxious, and isolated from the rest of the world and they feel like noone can understand what they are going through. PTSD short-circuits people's lives by causing disabling symptoms that include a hyper-alert nervous system, numbness and detachment, and intrusive thoughts or flashbacks about the trauma. So, what is trauma?

Dr. Goulston defines trauma by stating that it comes from the Greek word meaning, "wound". Trauma can wound the mind as well as the body. According to Dr. Goulston, there are four elements that define trauma; they are:

(1) it's an overwhelming event; large or small

(2) it threatens life and limb; either your own or that of someone you love

(3) it's unexpected

(4) it's an event that causes fear, helplessness, or horror in the person involved

In short, a trauma is a dangerous, shocking event that shakes both your body and your soul. It makes you fear for your life and your safety of the people you care about most and it breaks down your psychological defenses and shatters your sense of security.

Getting treatment if you have PTSD is crucial because this disorder does not simply go away on its own. PTSD involves profound biochemical and psychological changes that cause the toxic memories of a trauma to remain strong instead of fading. As a result, people with PTSD become trapped in their own trauma unable to process what happened and move on with their lives.

The good news is that PTSD is highly treatable and the vast majority of people with this disorder gain freedom from the disabling symptoms and get control of their lives again.

If any readers feel that they fit this profile, make an appointment to see your doctor right away and get a psychological assessment. More importantly, free yourself of the denial and the guilt. Recognize that you may indeed suffer from PTSD. Many readers may feel that PTSD is a cop-out. I had this nagging fear that fellow veterans, including my father (now deceased), would have this perception of me and, consequently, would be most ashamed of me.

Today, I continue to undergo therapy and treatment for PTSD and will continue to do so for a long time.

There are many resources to pursue regarding PTSD and I have listed some websites, just to name a few, that may be helpful to you as they have been for me. You will find these resources listed at the end of the book.

Whatever your circumstances may be and if you suffer from PTSD, get help today so you and your family can have a healthy, brighter tomorrow.

6 CONCLUSIONS

When all has been said and done, I often find myself still asking the same questions as I have been asking for the last thirty years, hoping to find the answers that will satisfy me. Such questions are:

Is it safe to assume that we, as Americans, are safe from future terrorist attacks?

Is it safe to assume that all our law enforcement agencies are cohesively and collectively working together as one entity (Homeland Security) to keep Americans safe from terrorism?

Is it safe to assume that we will not be kept in the dark, but instead, be provided the necessary tools to act accordingly should an attack occur?

Is it safe to assume we are safe? This is the most challenging question that requires the immediate attention of every American citizen, our state and local governments, and most importantly, our federal intelligence-gathering agencies.

Our fallen comrades, John Ball and Emil White, would surely like to see their children growing up in a country that is safe, secure and free. We owe it to these remarkable men to see to it that the tools to our way of life in America are never jeopardized nor taken for granted. Freedom is not free and we must not allow ourselves to become complacent to those elements out there who wish to undermine our lives.

None of us knows what the future will bring. Americans have always been a resilient people and we have learned to overcome many obstacles throughout our history. Hopefully, we have learned our lessons from the past and are now better equipped to meet the challenges of tomorrow. We are fully capable to face any adversaries who wish to undermine our will, our freedom and our spirit.

We may have lost some battles along the way, but one thing that has always amazed me about the American backbone is we have never lost a war!

God Bless America!!

RESOURCES

National Center for Post-traumatic Stress Disorder (PTSD)
(www.ncptsd.va.gov)
This site, created primarily for veterans and their families and for care providers, also provides excellent info for civilians dealing with PTSD. The site is a must-see if you are seeking basic information, whether you are a person with PTSD, a family member or friend, or a healthcare professional. It provides both basic information and loads of links to other sites, including excellent sites with info on helping children with PTSD. Another great feature: the PILOTS database, an electronic index to the worldwide with literature on PTSD.

If you are looking for other people who understand the pain of PTSD and who can offer both moral support and practical advice, the internet is a great place to find them. Here are good sites that can get you started:

PTSD Forum (www.ptsdform.org) is one of the best of the online discussion groups about PTSD.

American Self-Help Group Clearinghouse (mentalhelp.net/selfhelp) can help you find PTSD support groups in your area, whether you are battling PTSD yourself or you are a family member seeking ways to cope.

In you are serving your country right now or you wore a uniform in the past, check out these sites for information on the services available to you—and for moral support and practical advice from people who know the PTSD drill:

Military OneSource (www.militaryonesource.com) offers assistance in finding help for PTSD, for drug or alcohol problems, and for a wide range of other issues.

The Veterans' Coalition (www.theveteranscoalition. org) offers support and advice for people coping with PTSD and other post-combat issues.

Documentaries.

The Soldier's Heart, a PBS Frontline documentary available free of charge offers an in-depth look at the toll that PTSD takes on America's fighting forces.

Insights for Interventions: For Veterans and Families, a documentary narrated by Jane Pauley, is available free of charge on the website of the National Center for Post-traumatic Stress Disorder (PTSD). This program, which is one segment of a feature on women in the military, looks at the special problems of female veterans with PTSD and the treatment options that can benefit them.

Books.

Recovering from the War: A Guide for All Veterans, Family Members, Friends and Therapists, by Patience Mason (Patience Press, 1998)

Forgive for Good, by Frederic Luskin (HarperOne, 2003)

ACKNOWLEDGEMENTS

Carol Largman
Christine Leyba
Andrea Loveday
for
giving me the psychological, emotional support and the
encouragement to pursue this publication

Lynda Taylor
Michael Wilkinson
for
never losing faith in me

CTTCS Joseph Glockner
CTT2 Anthony Casey
for
sharing their resources and insights on this tragedy

The Cryptologic Community
Who demonstrated the kind of
Comraderie and "family" support that I have
yet to experience in any other profession

Daughter Britany Thornton
for
Her great assistance in typing this manuscript
John Stovall
And Family
For allowing me to publish this book from start to finish

<u>I LOVE YOU ALL</u>

BIBLIOGRAPHY

Goulston, Mark, M.D. <u>Post-Traumatic Stress Disorder for Dummies</u>. New Jersey: Wiley Publishing, Inc., 2008.

Kushner, Harvey W. <u>Encyclopedia of Terrorism</u>, California: Sage Publications, Inc., 2003.

New York Times. <u>A Nation Challenged: A Visual History of 9/11 and Its Aftermath</u>. Editors: Lee, Schlein, Levitas et al. New York: Calaway/Scholastic, 2002.

Outman, James and Elisabeth. <u>Terrorism Almanac</u>. Detroit: Thomson/Gale Group, 2003.

PHOTOGRAPHS

Lieutenant Orlando Gallardo, United States Navy
Senior Chief Petty Officer (CTOCS) Barry Hester, United States Navy
Petty Officer Second Class (CTA2) Jackie Polanco

WEBSITES

www.navycthistory.com
www.sabanaseca.navalspook-ctsandcrabs.us
     (Cryptologic Veteran's Notes)
Senior Chief Petty Officer (CTTCS) Joseph Glockner, United
     States Navy, retired (webmaster)